Roger Federer

www.pegasusforkids.com

© **B. Jain Publishers (P) Ltd.** All rights reserved. No part of this book may be reproduced, stored in a retrieval system or transmitted, in any form or by any means, mechanical, photocopying, recording or otherwise, without any prior written permission of the publisher.

Published by Kuldeep Jain for B. Jain Publishers (P) Ltd., D-157, Sector 63, Noida - 201307, U.P
Registered office: 1921/10, Chuna Mandi, Paharganj, New Delhi-110055

Printed in India

Contents

5   Who is Roger Federer?

8   Early Life and Personal History

20   Rising Star

36   Career Breakthrough

49   World Dominance

65   Legacy

68   Records, Awards and Recognition

72   Timeline

76   Activities

79   Glossary

Who is Roger Federer?

There are very few sportspersons who have achieved popularity for their sporting ability as well as their personalities, both in their home countries, and around the world. One such sportsman is Roger Federer.

Roger Federer was born on August 8, 1981 in the city of Basel in Switzerland. He is a professional tennis player, who is regarded by many as the greatest tennis player ever.

Federer is noted for his cool and calm nature and his impeccable manners on as well as off the court. Over the years, he has become more focused and calm even during difficult games. Experts believe this gives him an advantage over his less controlled opponents.

Federer turned professional in 1998 and has maintained his ranking among the top 10 in tennis since October 2002. Federer holds several records in the Open Era: World No. 1 position for 302 weeks (including 237 consecutive weeks); 19 Grand Slam singles titles; reaching each Grand Slam final at least five times (an all-time record); and reaching the Wimbledon final 10 times. He is among only eight men to ever capture a career Grand Slam. Federer shares the Open Era record for most titles at Wimbledon with Pete Sampras (seven) and at the US Open with Jimmy Connors (one) and Sampras (five). He is the only male player to have won five consecutive US Open titles.

His astonishing tennis records seem never-ending. He has won the most matches in Grand Slam events (307) and is the first player to record more than 65 wins at each Grand Slam tournament. Federer's ATP (Association of Tennis Professionals) tournament records include winning a record six ATP World Tour Finals, playing in the finals at all nine ATP Masters 1,000 tournaments (a record shared with Novak Djokovic and Rafael Nadal).

Federer also won the Olympic Gold Medal for doubles with his compatriot, Stan Wawrinka, at the 2008 Summer Olympic Games, and the Olympic Silver Medal in singles at the 2012 Summer Olympic Games. Representing Switzerland, he was part of the 2014 winning Davis Cup team. He finished eight consecutive years (2003–2010) at one of the top two positions in the year-end men's rankings and 10 years (2003–2012) in the top three. He was named the Laureus World Sportsman of the Year for a record four consecutive years (2005–2008).

In 2016, Federer was forced to take a six-month sabbatical due to a knee injury. Many people doubted if he would be able to return to the top of his form at 35 years of age, but he proved everyone wrong by defeating Rafael Nadal to win the Australian Open in 2017.

It is because of his hunger for success, his incredible hard work and talent, and remarkable levels of consistency that Roger Federer has emerged as possibly the best tennis player in the sport's history.

Early Life and Personal History

Roger Federer was born at the Basel Cantonal Hospital in Basel, Switzerland, on August 8, 1981. His father, Robert Federer, is Swiss from Berneck, near the border between Switzerland, Austria and Germany, while his mother,

Lynette Federer, comes from Kempton Park, Gauteng, and is a South African whose ancestors were Dutch and French Huguenots. Because of this, Federer holds both Swiss and South African citizenship. Federer has just one sibling—his older sister, Diana, who is the mother to a set of twins.

Federer may be a popular sports figure, but he is quite tight-lipped when it comes to talking about his family life. He makes it a point to keep his private life away from the media glare. Federer is married to former Women's Tennis Association player, Mirka Vavrinec. He met her while both were competing for Switzerland in the 2000

Sydney Olympics. Vavrinec retired from professional tennis in 2002 because of a foot injury. They got married at Wenkenhof Villa in Riehen, a place close to where Federer grew up in Basel, on April 11, 2009. Only close family and friends were part of their wedding ceremony. In July 2009, Mirka gave birth to identical twin girls, Myla

Rose and Charlene Riva. The couple had another set of twins in 2014, this time boys whom they named Leo and Lennart (Lenny).

Federer grew up near Birsfelden, Riehen, and then Münchenstein, close to the French and German borders, and speaks Swiss German, Standard German, English and

French fluently. Swiss German is his native language. His family was very religious and he was raised as a Roman Catholic. Because of his religious upbringing, one of the most defining moments for Federer was when he met Pope Benedict XVI while playing the 2006 Internazionali BNL d'Italia tournament in Rome.

Like all male citizens of Switzerland, Roger too was supposed to appear for compulsory military service in the Swiss Armed Forces. However, in 2003 he was ruled 'unsuitable' and was not required to fulfil his military obligations. Instead, he served in the civil protection force and was required to pay three% of his taxable income as an alternative.

Although he went on to become one of the best tennis players ever, Roger grew up as an ardent football fan. He was a staunch supporter of FC Basel and the Swiss National Football Team. Federer credits the wide range of sports he played as a child—he also played badminton and basketball—for his hand-eye coordination.

Roger Federer is in many ways, an unlikely tennis champion. While his parents were keen players, they didn't force young Roger to spend hours drilling on the court as many 'tennis parents' do. It was pure talent that earned him a spot in Basel's Old Boys Tennis Club, where he received his first formal instruction in the sport as an eight-year-old.

When Federer was 12 years old, he realised that attaining his sporting ambitions to be the best tennis player would require a lot of focus and sacrifice. Despite being skilled at skiing and an avid footballer, he chose to focus all his energy and time on tennis, so that he could rise to the next level. At this time, he teamed up with Peter Carter from Australia, who had a great impact on the temperament

and technique of young Federer. Besides teaching Federer a disciplined approach to selecting shots, Carter helped the young Swiss player to understand that emotional reactions during a game would drain out his energy and cost him valuable points on the court. This brought about a remarkable change and maturity in Federer's attitude on court, even though at that time he was still a few years away from gaining his characteristic calm demeanour.

Roger made a very tough decision as a 14 year-old adolescent, when he opted to move from Basel to Lausanne, to attend Switzerland's National Training Centre. This was a two-hour train ride from his home, so he did manage to make weekend trips to visit his parents and siblings. However, living away from home took a toll on the teenager. He was further isolated because he could not speak French fluently, which alienated him from his peers. While many others at his age would have been disheartened, it was not so with young Roger. This phase was a defining one for him, both as a player and an individual. He realised that talent alone would not help him succeed; he needed to stay positive and work hard. Overcoming these struggles and challenges proved to be good for him, and helped him develop into a more mature and driven person at an early age.

Rising Star

Despite the hardships and problems he had to face, the move to the Swiss National Training Centre did wonders for Federer. It helped him to improve as a player and also grow as a person.

After a few years at the National Training Centre, Federer enrolled at a new training centre in Biel, where he once again got to train with Peter Carter. The pair found that they still shared a strong bond, and they continued to work together closely as Federer rose through the junior ranks.

In 1998, under the additional guidance of former Swedish player Peter Lundgren, Federer won the Junior Wimbledon singles and doubles titles, the prestigious Orange Bowl

championship, and reached the final of the US Open. He finished the year as the top-ranked junior player in the world.

His early success at the junior level brought with it a lot of pressure and attention. However, Federer had a very sensible outlook to this new popularity. He was aware that early success may not always translate into triumph later in life, and thus he took some very intelligent steps as he prepared to start his senior career. He hired Lundgren as his full-time coach, and they planned out a smart schedule that alternated between main draw ATP (Association of Tennis Professionals) events and Challenger tournaments.

In 1999, boosted by quarter-finals showings at events in Basel, Marseille and Rotterdam, he became the youngest player in the ATP's top 100. The following years saw Roger build steadily on his initial senior success. In 2000, he reached the ATP Final for the first time in Marseille, unfortunately losing out to Marc Rosset by a narrow margin in a third set tie-break. For the first time at Roland Garros, Federer reached the last 16 of a Grand Slam, narrowly missing out on a bronze medal win at the Sydney Olympics. His home fans were elated when he won the showpiece match in Basel, ending the year with an impressive rank 29. Federer had clearly outlined his ambitions in the sport in just his second full year as a senior professional.

The following year, Federer consistently rose in the world rankings and constantly proved his potential as a rising future tennis star. After winning his first title in Milan, he went on to reach the first Grand Slam quarter

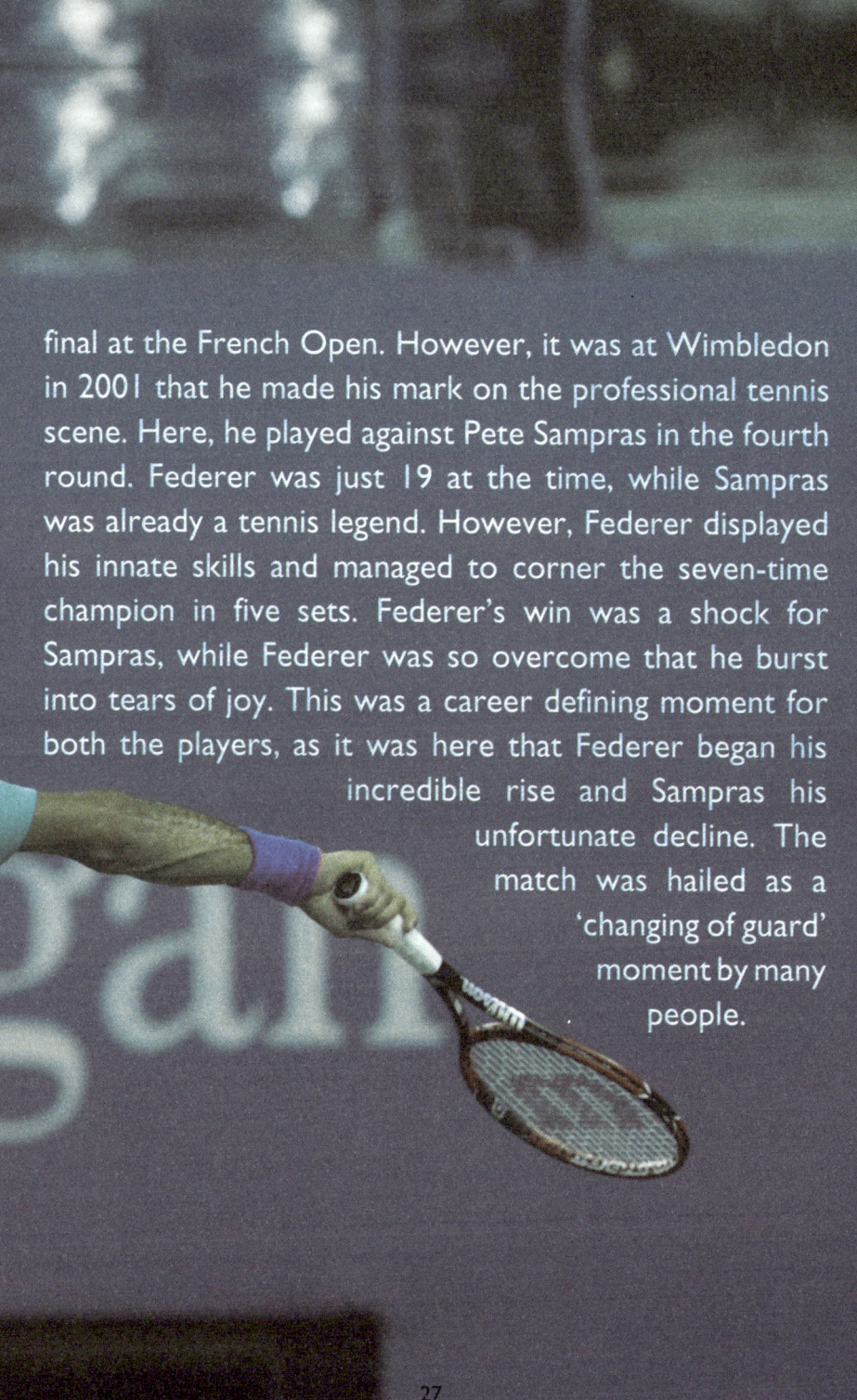

final at the French Open. However, it was at Wimbledon in 2001 that he made his mark on the professional tennis scene. Here, he played against Pete Sampras in the fourth round. Federer was just 19 at the time, while Sampras was already a tennis legend. However, Federer displayed his innate skills and managed to corner the seven-time champion in five sets. Federer's win was a shock for Sampras, while Federer was so overcome that he burst into tears of joy. This was a career defining moment for both the players, as it was here that Federer began his incredible rise and Sampras his unfortunate decline. The match was hailed as a 'changing of guard' moment by many people.

Despite this incredible game and a few others like this, Federer's progress was slowed down by injuries and loss of form. This inconsistency continued for much of the following year. While there were many highlights, including a tournament win in Sydney and his first Masters Series final in Miami, it appeared as if Federer was struggling to cope with the pressure of increased expectations. He continued to follow up impressive wins with surprising, disheartening losses. For example, after winning his first

Masters title in Hamburg, he crashed out of the French Open in the first round. Four weeks later, defending quarter-finals points at the All England Club, he lost to 154th-ranked Mario Ancic, also in the first round. He had been seen as a title contender at the start of

the 2002 Wimbledon, but Federer's early exit prompted the belief that, while he undoubtedly had the talent to succeed, he lacked the necessary mental toughness. When he won only one of his next five matches, the critics grew louder.

It was then that Roger's life underwent a major shift, due to a terrible tragedy. In 2001, Federer was at a tournament in Toronto, when he learnt that Peter Carter, his old coach, had died in a car accident. Federer, who had been very close to Carter, was very upset. The tragedy made him introspect and recall the lessons his former mentor had instilled in him, especially the importance of hard work, meticulous preparation, and a balanced, positive attitude. This helped Federer rethink his entire approach to the

game, and infused him with a new sense of dedication. Federer emerged stronger and with a renewed focus, he managed to end his string of losses with a fourth round appearance at the US Open. In that year, he smoothly navigated through three quarter-finals, a semi-final in Basel, and went on to win the title in Vienna.

Ranked 6th in the world, he qualified for the elite end-of-year ATP Championships, won the first three matches and pushed then world number 1 Lleyton Hewitt to the limit in a thrilling semi-final. He ended the year a more

emotionally mature man and a tougher, more resilient player. He had set his sights on what he wanted to achieve and now had developed the right mindset along with the talent, will, and tenacity to fulfil his dreams.

Towards the beginning of the season in 2003, Federer was determined to take home his first Grand Slam title.

He had already lost out on a five-setter at the Australian Open to his erstwhile junior rival David Nalbandian, but managed to reach the top 5 for the first time after winning in Dubai and Marseille. However, Federer lost out the first round to journeyman Luis Homa at Roland Garros. This development made sceptics and fans believe that this might be yet another setback.

Federer recovered two times in Halle, from losing the opening set to win the championship. While at Wimbledon, he lost only one set out of the first four matches he played, and also managed to recover from a terrible back strain to make it to the semi-finals. Those who were not privy to Federer's potential started recognizing his true calibre and hailing him as a distinguished tennis player and a strong competitor who knew all the tricks of the trade to become a winner. Federer's game was so strong that it made his opponents seem weak and their style of play simplistic.

Career Breakthrough

With his first Grand Slam win at Wimbledon, Roger finished the 2003 season at a career high world no. 2 behind Andy Roddick of USA. Thus, 2003 turned out to be the year Federer entered the highest level.

In 2004, Roger Federer had one of the most successful years in the Open Era of modern men's tennis. He won three of the four Grand Slam singles tournaments; did not lose a match to anyone ranked in the top 10; he won every final he reached, and was named the ITF Tennis

World Champion. His win–loss record for the year was 74–6 with 11 titles, which included three of the year's four Grand Slams and three ATP Masters Series titles.

Winning three Grand Slams for the first time in his career was a huge milestone for Federer. In fact, he was the first player to win three Grand Slams in a single season since Mats Wilander in 1988. The first came at the Australian Open where Federer defeated Marat Safin, 7–6(3), 6–4, 6–2. He went on to win his second Wimbledon crown over Andy Roddick, 4–6, 7–5, 7–6(3), 6–4. In addition, Federer defeated the 2001 US Open Champion Lleyton

Hewitt at the US Open, to win his first US Open title, 6–0, 7–6(3), 6–0. Federer also won three ATP Masters 1,000 events, one on clay at Hamburg, and two on hard court in Indian Wells and Canada. Federer took home the ATP 500 series title at Dubai, and wrapped up the year with a second win over Lleyton Hewitt at the Tennis Masters Cup. Federer became the first man in the Open Era to win at least three Grand Slams and the Year-End Championships. As of 2015, Federer and Novak Djokovic are the only male tennis players to have accomplished

this, with Federer repeating the feat in 2006 and 2007, and Djokovic achieving this in 2015.

Federer entered the 2004 Australian Open as the second seed behind American Andy Roddick. In the fourth round, he rallied to defeat former number one Lleyton Hewitt after dropping the first set. His rival David Nalbandian, who had won five of their six previous meetings, awaited him in the quarterfinals. Federer managed to defeat the Argentine in four tight sets.

The semi-finals proved easier, as Federer easily defeated world no. 3 Juan Carlos Ferrero and reached his first Australian Open final. His opponent in the final was former world no. 1 and 2000 US Open champion Marat Safin.

After winning the opening set in a tiebreaker Federer secured a 7–6, 6–4, 6–2 championship win. This victory won him his first Australian Open and his second career

Grand Slam. This win also saw him emerge as the new world no. 1 on February 2, 2004, a ranking he would hold for an all-time record 237 consecutive weeks until August 18, 2008.

He now travelled to play at the Masters Competition in Indian Wells, California. Here, he came face to face with American legend Andre Agassi in the semi-finals. Agassi won the first set, but Federer rallied to win a spot in the finals. Once again, he had defeated a tennis legend, which made more and more tennis fans and spectators take notice of his ability. Federer then made the most of the opportunity at hand by defeating Tim Henman in straight sets to win the title, at the 2004 Pacific Life Open.

Federer now entered the Wimbledon Championships as the defending champion. He was aiming to be the first man to defend his title at Wimbledon since Pete Sampras (1999–2000). The Swiss lost only one set in all his matches as he made his way to the final. Here he played against world number 2 Andy Roddick for the championship in a thrilling four set final. Roddick came out strong with incredible serves, and took the first set. The second set began with Federer racing out to a 4–0 lead, but Roddick rallied to level it at 4–4. Federer ultimately broke Roddick in the twelfth game and levelled the match at one set apiece. The crucial third set was decided by a tiebreaker which was won by the Swiss defending champion. Federer thus finally closed out the match in four sets to win his third career Grand Slam.

Federer's first tournament after Wimbledon was the Swiss Open at Gstaad. This was a clay court tournament that Federer played because it was a major tournament in his country. He had played Gstaad every year between 1998 and 2003, but had never won. That changed in 2004. He defeated Igor Andreev to win a tournament in Switzerland for the first time in his career.

His 23-match winning streak shockingly ended in the first round of the Cincinnati Masters where Federer was upset by Slovakian player Dominik Hrbaty. Next, Federer entered the Athens Olympics as the top-seeded player and was considered the crowd favourite, but he was upset in the second round by Czech teenager and future world number 4, Tomáš Berdych. This was the last loss Federer suffered for the remainder of his 2004 season.

Federer entered the 2004 US Open as the top seed, looking to win his first US Open championship. Federer cruised through the first four rounds before facing Andre Agassi in the quarterfinals. His match against the two-time US Open champion proved to be a thrilling five-set epic, which Federer won. In the semi-finals, Federer eased past Tim Henman in straight sets. Federer then won his first US Open singles title, defeating Lleyton Hewitt, 6–0, 7–6(3), 6–0, in the final. This was one of the most dominant displays in US Open history, as Roger Federer was the first player to win two 'bagel sets' in the final since 1884.

Federer made it to two Grand Slam finals in 2005, winning both, at Wimbledon over Andy Roddick, 6–2, 7–6(2), 6–4, and then defeating Andre Agassi in his last Grand Slam final at the US Open, 6–3, 2–6, 7–6(1), 6–1. However, Federer failed to make it to the final at the other two majors, losing in the semi-final of the Australian Open to Marat Safin and at the French Open to Spaniard Rafael Nadal. Nevertheless, Federer won four ATP Masters Series 1000 at Indian Wells, Miami, and Cincinnati on hard courts and one lone clay court title at Hamburg. Furthermore, Federer also won two ATP 500 series events at Rotterdam and Dubai. Even though he lost the Year-End Championships to David Nalbandian in the final, Roger's 2005 season was

statistically one of the most dominant in the Open Era. In a sense, he redefined tennis with his extraordinary displays. He won 11 singles titles which tied his 2004 season as the most in over two decades, his 81 match victories were the most since Pete Sampras in 1993, and his record of 81-4 (95.2%) remains the second best winning percentage in the Open Era behind only John McEnroe in 1984. These incredible performances well and truly established Roger Federer as one of the strongest players in the history of tennis.

World Dominance

The year 2006 proved to be an even better season for Federer. In fact, it was Federer's best season as a professional tennis player as well as one of the best in the sport's history. This period also saw the intensification of his on-court rivalry with the Spaniard Rafael Nadal,

against whom he was pitted time and again in some of the most exciting and hard-fought tennis matches.

In December 2011, Stephen Tignor, chief editorial writer for Tennis.com, ranked Federer's 2006 season as the second-greatest season of all time during the Open Era, right behind Rod Laver's Grand Slam year of 1969. In this year, Federer won 12 singles titles (the most of any player since John McEnroe in 1984) and had a match record of 92–5 (the most wins since Ivan Lendl in 1982). Federer reached the finals in an astounding 16 of the 17 tournaments he entered during the season. Further, in the 2006 season, Federer won three of the four Grand Slam titles, only being defeated by Rafael Nadal in the French Open. Federer also became

the first man to reach all four finals in a calendar year since Rod Laver in 1969.

Federer defeated his rival Rafael Nadal in the Wimbledon Championships final. In the Australian Open, Federer triumphed over Marcos Baghdatis, and at the US Open, he defeated 2003 winner Andy Roddick. In addition, Federer made it to six ATP Masters Series 1000 finals, winning four on hard surfaces and losing two on clay to Nadal.

However, Federer regularly pushed Nadal to the limit on clay throughout the season, taking him to fourth-set tiebreakers in Monte Carlo and Paris, and an incredible game in Rome that went to a deciding fifth-set tiebreaker. Federer won one ATP 500 series event in Tokyo and captured the year-end championships for the third time in his career, once again finishing the year as world No. 1, thereby continuing an era of absolute dominance.

Federer only lost to two players during 2006—to Nadal four times in finals, and to 19-year-old Andy Murray in the second round of the 2006 Cincinnati Masters, in

what would be Federer's only defeat before the final that year. Federer finished the season on a stunning 29-match winning streak, as well as winning 48 of his last 49 matches after the French Open, a feat which once again cemented his status as the best player on the planet and arguably in the history of the sport. A personal highlight for

Federer came near the end of the season when he finally won his hometown tournament, the Swiss Indoors in Basel, Switzerland.

The year 2007 proved just as successful for Federer, who yet again reached four Grand Slam finals, winning three of them. Federer had entered the year on a huge winning streak and after capturing his fourth Dubai crown Federer's winning streak stood at an amazing 41 matches,

the longest of his career and only five shy of the world record. During the clay season, Federer's victory in the Hamburg Masters final was particularly impressive, as it snapped Nadal's mind boggling 81-match winning streak on clay, an Open Era record.

At the French Open, some anticipated that Federer could become the first man in almost 40 years to hold all four majors simultaneously, having just thoroughly defeated rival Nadal on clay. However, in a repeat of the previous year, Federer played a difficult four-set final against Nadal, but was beaten by going 1/18 on break-point chances.

At Wimbledon, Federer entered the tournament not only as the four-time defending champion, but also riding a 48-match winning streak on the grass surface. Once again, he defeated Nadal for a second consecutive year in the final, this time in a thrilling five-set encounter that many experts hailed as the greatest Wimbledon final since 1980. With his fifth title at Wimbledon, Roger equalled Swedish legend Bjorn Borg's record of five consecutive titles at the prestigious tournament.

Roger Federer finished as the year-end world No. 1 for the fourth year in a row, demonstrating his brilliance at the game. During these four years, he won 11 Grand Slam singles titles. After his incredible triple Grand Slam season, yet again, Federer became the only player in history to win three Majors titles in a year for three years (2004, 2006, 2007). It was also the third consecutive season that Federer held the world No. 1 ranking for all 52 weeks of the year.

Aside from his professional matches, Roger represented his country at the Olympics. At the 2008 Olympic Games held in Beijing, China, Roger Federer and Stan Wawrinka won the Gold Medal in doubles, after beating the Bryan brothers from the American team in the semi-final and the Swedish duo of Simon Aspelin and Thomas Johansson in the final. However, Federer did not experience the same success in the singles format, where he was knocked out in the quarterfinals by the then No.8 ranked James Blake.

The 2009 season was perhaps Federer's most historic season as he completed a career Grand Slam, finally winning his first French Open title. He also won a record 15th Grand Slam singles title by defeating Andy Roddick at Wimbledon in five sets, beating Pete Sampras' record of fourteen Grand Slam singles trophies. The 2009 Wimbledon final was also historic for being the longest Grand Slam final in terms of games played, with Federer prevailing 16–14 in a thrilling fifth set. The stamina and

endurance he displayed during this hard-fought game, in the midst of immense stress truly showed his class and demonstrated once again why he is considered the best.

While he remained a strong player, the rise of talented younger players like Novak Djokovic, as well as physical issues and loss of form resulted in Federer losing his dominant position in the following years. In 2016, he had to take almost six months off from the game due to a knee injury, and many thought that it would be impossible for him to return to the same high level of performance as before. However, in 2017, Roger Federer stunned and delighted spectators the world over, when at the age of 35, he powered through to the finals of the Australian Open, where he once again faced his long-time opponent, Rafael Nadal.

Federer's win in the 2017 Australian Open against Nadal is a victory that has gone down in the history of sporting events. This was the first time that Federer managed to defeat Nadal at a Grand Slam other than Wimbledon. With this win, Federer expanded his singles titles scores to a remarkable 18, breaking his own previous record. After the win, the moniker 'Fedal XXXV' was coined, putting together the names of both opponents—Federer and Nadal.

Soon after, Federer created history once again, winning two American hard-court Masters events—Indian Wells and Miami. This was the first time after 2006 that he won the first three biggest tennis tournaments of the season.

At Miami, he once again defeated Rafael Nadal in a hard fought battle.

His comeback victory was even more remarkable since he had not won a Major in the last five years, and had only managed two titles in his last 26 appearances at these three events! As always, Federer credited his friends, family, and his coaching staff for his long and successful playing career.

Legacy

Federer is not only a very popular sportsperson, but also one of the most successful ones. He has prevailed on both grass and clay courts, and has impressed critics, fans, as well as past and present players.

He has more Grand Slam tournament titles (19 as on December 2017) than any other men's singles player. He spent the most amount of time in the Open Era at the top

of the ATP Rankings (302 weeks). He also holds the record for the most titles (6) at the year-end tournament, where only the year-end 8 highest-ranked players participate. Federer has been ranked among the top 8 players in the world continuously since October 14, 2002.

Other than his match wins, Federer has also won the ATPWorldTour.com Fans' Favourite Award a record 13 times consecutively (2003–2015) and the Stefan Edberg Sportsmanship Award (voted for by players) a record 11 times (2004–2009, 2011–2015), both awards indicative of the respect and popularity he enjoys. He also won the Arthur Ashe Humanitarian of the Year Award twice, in 2006 and 2013. He was named the Laureus World Sportsman of the Year for a record four consecutive years (2005–2008).

Federer is at times referred to as the 'Federer Express', shortened to 'Fed Express' or 'FedEx', and the 'Swiss Maestro', or just 'Maestro'. It is because of players like Roger Federer that the standards and importance of tennis has reached great heights in the recent years.

Federer has achieved all the awards and honours there are to win in tennis. He has also gained popularity and world-wide affection for his humanitarian work. He has established his own organisation, the Roger Federer Foundation, to help children in need around the world and provide them with health care, food and education. He is also the UNICEF's Goodwill Ambassador. His incredibly giving nature as a person, as well as his professional dedication, hard work and skill on the tennis court makes Federer a 'Maestro' in the true sense of the word.

Records, Awards and Recognition

Roger Federer has amassed a staggering number of awards in the course of his tennis career. He has been counted amongst the most talented, successful, and one of the richest sportspersons. He has created and broken numerous tennis records, of which some of the major ones have been listed here.

Records:

- 19 Grand Slam men singles titles.
- All four Grand Slam finals in one season, three times (2006–2007 & 2009).
- Two men's Grand Slam titles per year five times (2004–07 & 2009).
- 10 consecutive men's Grand Slam finals (2005–2007).
- 65 men's Grand Slam tournament appearances in a row.
- 10 finals at a single Grand Slam tournament (Wimbledon).
- Won first seven Grand Slam finals
- Fastest player to win 15 Grand Slams in six years.

Other Records:

- 2004–2010, 2012: 302 total weeks at no. 1

- 2003–2005: 26 consecutive match victories vs. top 10 opponents
- 2003–2006: Won Halle Open and Wimbledon for four consecutive years
- 1999–2016: 668 hard court match victories overall
- 2005–2006: 56 consecutive hard court match victories
- 17 ATP 500 Series titles
- 1999, 2004, 2008, 2012: 13 Olympic Match wins
- 2000, 2001, 2006–2015: 12 finals at a single tournament (Swiss Indoors)
- Highest overall grass court match win percentage: 86.86% (152–23)

Awards;

- ITF World Junior Champion: 1998
- ATP European Player of the Year: 2003, 2004
- ATP Player of the Year: 2004, 2005, 2006, 2007, 2008, 2010
- Swiss Sportsman of the Year: 2003, 2004, 2006, 2007, 2012, 2014
- Swiss of the Year: 2003

Records, Awards and Recognition

- Michael-Westphal Award: 2003, 2005
- ATPTennis.com Fans' Favourite award: 2004, 2005, 2006, 2007, 2008
- ATPWorldtour.com (formerly ATPTennis.com) Fans' Favourite (for the year 2008): 2009, 2010, 2011, 2012, 2013, 2014, 2015
- ITF World Champion: 2004
- Sports Illustrated Tennis Player of the Year: 2004
- Reuters International Sportsman of the Year: 2004
- BBC Overseas Sports Personality of the Year: 2004, 2006, 2007
- International Tennis Writers Association (ITWA) Player of the Year: 2004, 2005, 2006
- Golden Bagel Award: 2004, 2006
- European Sportsman of the Year (aka UEPS [Federation of European sports journalists] Sportsman of the Year): 2004, 2005, 2008, 2009
- Ambassador of United Nations' Year of Sport and Physical Education: 2005
- Goldene Kamera Award: 2005
- Stefan Edberg Sportsmanship Award: 2005,

2006, 2007, 2008, 2009, 2010, 2011, 2012, 2013, 2014, 2015

- Laureus World Sportsman of the Year: 2005, 2006, 2007, 2008

- International Tennis Writers Ambassador for Tennis: 2005, 2006

- ITF World Champion: 2005, 2006, 2007, 2009

- ESPY Best Male Tennis Player: 2005, 2006, 2007, 2008, 2009, 2010

- The Prix Orange Award: 2005, 2006, 2007, 2008, 2009

- Arthur Ashe Humanitarian of the Year: 2007, 2013

- Olympic Men's Doubles Gold Medallist at the 2008 Olympic Games

- Ehrespalebaerglemer Award: An award given to outstanding citizens of the city of Basel: 2009

- ATPWorldtour.com Player of the Decade: 2009

- Best Grand Slam/Davis Cup Match of the Year: 2011

- Olympics Singles Silver Medallist at 2012 Olympic Games.

Timeline

- **1981** Born in Basel, Switzerland on August 8, 1981

- **1998** Won both the singles and doubles title at Junior Wimbledon; played his first tournament as a professional tennis player in Gstaad; ended the year ranked no.1 in the Junior World Rankings.

- **1999** Entered the top 100 rankings as a professional for the first time

- **2000** Played his first tournament final in the Marseille Cup

- **2001** Made his first quarter-final appearance in a Grand Slam at the French Open; memorably defeated Pete Sampras in quarter-final of Wimbledon Championships

- **2002** Won his first Master Series event at the Hamburg Masters; ranked among the top ten players in the world for the first time, at no.6.

- **2003** Won his first Grand Slam title at the Wimbledon Championships; won seven of the nine ATP tour finals he played;

defeated Andre Agassi to finish the year ranked world no.2.

- **2004** Won three Grand Slam titles in a year for the first time in his career; became first person to do so since Mats Wilander in 1988; won the Australian Open, Wimbledon Championships and the US Open; won the Swiss Open in Gstaad, held in his native country, for the first time; ended the year ranked World no.1 for the first time in his career.

- **2005** Won the Wimbledon Championships and the USOpen.

- **2006** Won 12 singles titles in a year; became the first man to reach all four Grand Slam finals since Rod Laver in 1969; won the Australian Open, the Wimbledon Championship, the US Open.

- **2007** Won the Australian Open, the Wimbledon Championship and the US Open; named ATP Player of The Year, Arthur Ashe Humanitarian of the Year, Laureus World Sportsman of the Year;

Timeline

ended the year ranked as the no. 1 tennis player in the world.

- 2008 Won the US Open; won the Olympic Gold Medal in the doubles category; named Laureus World Sportsman of the Year.

- 2009 Married Mirka Vavrinec, who gave birth to twin daughters; completed a career Grand Slam; won the French Open, the Wimbledon Championship; named as one of Sports Illustrated's Athletes of the Decade.

- 2010 Won the Australian Open.

- 2011 Won a record sixth ATP World Tour Finals title; won the Swiss Indoors; won the Paris Masters.

- 2012 Won the Wimbledon Championships; won the Olympic Silver Medal in the singles category; listed at no. 1 in 100 Greatest of All Time by Tennis Channel; named Swiss Sportsman of the Year.

- 2013 Won the Gerry Weber Open; awarded Stefan Edberg Sportsmanship Award; named Arthur Ashe Humanitarian of the Year.

- 2014 His twin sons were born; won the Davis Cup for Switzerland for the first time in the country's history; awarded US Open Sportsmanship Award; named Swiss Sportsman of the Year; named as Davis Cup Most Valuable Player (shared with Stan Wawrinka).

- 2015 Became only the third player in the history of the sport to win one thousand matches; won the Gerry Weber Open; won the Swiss Indoors; awarded the Stefan Edberg Sportsmanship Award.

- 2016 Sustained knee injury, causing a forced sabbatical for the second half of the year.

- 2017 Won the Australian Open. Won the Indian Wells and Miami Masters events.

Activities

Group Activity

- Make a presentation or collage of your favourite tennis player.
- Learn and research about the different types of tournaments in tennis.
- Find out which tennis tournaments are played in your country.
- What are the rules of playing tennis? In groups, present these rules to your classmates in creative ways, such as through posters, models, PowerPoint presentations, etc.

Class Discussion

- What is the importance of sports in our lives?
- Discuss the topic: What is the importance of having a national sport? What kind of support should the government give to make sports more popular?
- Some sports like tennis require special equipment like racquets, nets and balls, can be expensive. How can such sports be made more accessible to talented people who may not be able to afford these costs?

Questions

1. Where and when was Roger Federer born?
2. How many siblings does Roger Federer have?
3. What is the name of Roger Federer's wife?
4. How many children does Roger Federer have?
5. In which year did Roger Federer win his first junior title?
6. Which was Roger Federer's first major junior title win?
7. In which year did Roger Federer turn professional?
8. When did Roger Federer enter the world's top 100 rankings for the first time in his career?
9. In which year did Roger Federer play his first final in a tournament as a professional tennis player? What was the name of the tournament?
10. When did Roger Federer win his first Grand Slam title? What was the name of the tournament he won?
11. Name Roger Federer's first ever coach. How did he affect Roger's development?

Activities

12. When was Roger Federer first named as the number 1 tennis player?

13. In which year did Roger Federer complete a career Grand Slam?

15. What was Roger Federer's longest winning streak?

16. How did Roger Federer overcome his over expressive behaviour on the tennis court as a professional?

17. Which player did Roger Federer defeat to win his only French Open title? In which year did he do so?

18. How many singles titles has Roger Federer won?

19. How do we know Roger Federer is interested in humanitarian work?

20. Who was Roger Federer's partner in the doubles category when he won the Gold Medal in the 2008 Beijing Olympics?

ATP: acronym for Association of Tennis Professionals. It is the main body for men's professional tennis and governs the ATP World Tour.

bagel: term that indicates winning or losing a set 6–0. The zero shape is similar to the round shape of a bagel.

backhand: a stroke where the ball is hit with the back face of the racket

career Grand Slam: players who win all four Major tournaments in their career have a Career Grand Slam

Davis Cup: an annual international men's tennis competition. Teams from participating countries compete in a single-elimination format.

deuce: a score of 40–40 in a game

doubles: a match played by 4 players, 2 on each side of the court. A doubles court is 9 ft wider than a singles court.

Golden Bagel Award: award given to male players winning the most bagels (sets won 6–0). Davis Cup matches and incomplete sets are not counted.

Grand Slam: winning all four of the prestigious major tournaments in a calendar year. It may

Glossary

also refer to any one of the four tournaments: the Australian Open, the French Open (Roland Garros), Wimbledon, and the US Open.

ITF: acronym for International Tennis Federation. It is the governing body of world tennis, and was earlier known as the International Lawn Tennis Federation (ILTF), founded in 1913.

Masters Cup: the year-end ATP championship, in which the eight highest-ranked players compete in a round-robin format, was earlier known as the Masters Cup

Open Era: the period in tennis since 1968, when tournaments became open to both amateurs and professional players